RELATIONSHIPS

6 Dramatic Monologues

3 for men
3 for women

Running time for each monologue
7 - 20 minutes

TSL Drama

Published in Great Britain in 2018
By TSL (Drama) Publications, Rickmansworth

Copyright © 2018

Images courtesy of https://pixabay.com/en/smartphone-hand-photo-montage-faces-1445489/

ISBN / 978-1-912416-31-8

Rights of performance

Contents

	Age Guide	page
Monologues for Men		
Hostile witness	45	5
Julia Underwood		
Wenglish	40-ish	11
David Stroud		
The waiting man	55	18
Stephen Baker		
Monologues for Women		
A true gentleman	70	29
John Samson		
Kenneth	Middle-aged	36
Barbara Towell		
Football results	50s	49
Melville Lovatt		

4

A stakeout in a restaurant

Hostile Witness

by

Julia Underwood

2nd place, Harrow Writers' Circle Monologue Competition
2017

Setting

Evening.

Man of 45, seated.

He has a black eye and one arm in a sling.

Performance time:

10 minutes

You'll be wondering how I got these injuries. I should take the blame because it was all my idea. The Gov said something like: 'Use you initiative, Barry' in a tone that suggested I didn't have any, so I went for it.

Pause.

The witness wasn't very keen – a bit of a shrinking violet – but I talked her into it.

'Will it be dangerous?' she asked, all shy and sweet.

I reassured her that I'd be there the whole time – some of the lads too – there was nothing to worry about.

'All right, I'll do it,' she said, meek as anything.

Pause.

It was one of those huge restaurants. The kind they use for wedding venues and Masonic dinners. Not my idea of a place for a romantic rendezvous, but it was where the suspect was coming so we had to be there.

I'd told the witness to dress up and I must say she scrubbed up well. I couldn't fault her black cocktail dress and high heels. I almost didn't recognise her with her hair up when I collected her.

'You look nice,' I muttered, thinking a compliment might relax her.

'Is that appropriate,' she asked as if I'd insulted her, 'in the circumstances?'

We sat at a table in the centre with a view of the entrance so we'd spot the suspect as she came in. Parsons and Taylor were at a table near the window looking ridiculous in their best suits. Parsons, not known for his sartorial taste, wore an outfit that would've looked better on the bouncer of a strip joint.

I looked round at the fancy decoration. The place reeked of money. The menu confirmed that the boss's budget would take a hammering if we actually ate there.

'You like-a a drink?' asked the waiter in a thick Mediterranean accent.

'Oh, yes,' piped up the witness before I had a chance to say no. 'Gin and tonic please.'

I didn't intend to drink as it might look bad later, so I ordered a sparkling water with lemon as if I'd copied my companion.

'It's very grand,' she said. 'How do you know she'll be coming here?'

'We've been listening to her phone for weeks,' I said, it couldn't matter telling her now. 'Don't be nervous.'

'I find it a bit intimidating,' she said, 'with the chandeliers and the fancy gold paint. I'm not nervous.'

'Then stop fiddling with the cutlery. I suppose you'd feel more at home at the Dog and Duck.'

'There's no need to be rude.'

That sounded huffy, so I shut up.

The waiter arrived with our drinks, making a fuss.

'There, signora,' he said with greasy grin. 'Lovely gin and tonic-a. Enjoy-a.' He leant too close, in my opinion. He addressed me with less charm. 'You have chosen from menu, signor?'

'Not yet. We're waiting for friends so may not order till they're here.'

The man shrugged and stalked off to the kitchen.

The witness took a sip of gin and I noticed her hand shook. Poor woman's proper scared, I thought.

'Thank goodness he's gone; I don't want to block your view of the entrance. She should be here by now, but women are often late.'

'Isn't she meeting someone?'

'Yes. Look, try not to be too obvious. If she knows the place is staked out she'll make a run for it. If we lose this chance to identify her we may never get another.'

'I know it's important,' she said, 'but I don't do this kind of thing every day.' She tensed, 'I think she's coming in now. I don't remember her being so tall.'

I looked at the woman coming down the steps to the dining area. She was tall, but that would be the five-inch heels. Her long blonde hair hung in a glowing curtain around her bare shoulders. She wore a slinky, strapless gown down to the floor. It left nothing to the imagination.

'That's a beautiful frock,' the witness said.

'This isn't a fashion show. Just tell me. Is it her?'

'I don't remember all that blonde hair. Oh dear, I'm not sure. Yes, I'm pretty certain it is, but it was dark.'

'You already told me that. So, is it the woman in the alley on the night of the murder? Can we make an arrest?'

'That's up to you,' she said. 'You're the policeman.'

'OK. When I stand up, you stay there. I'll signal the others.'

Pause.

That's when it all went pear-shaped. I stood up to approach the suspect, feeling triumphant, and a horrified expression crossed her face.

Then something happened that floored me, literally. She drew a gun from nowhere. One of those tiny automatics – she must've had it strapped to her ankle because there's nowhere she could have hidden it in that dress.

I was on the floor by the table and my witness, more quick-witted than I would have expected, turned our table on its side. The drinks, cutlery and tablecloth fell in a messy heap on the carpet.

Somewhere behind me I heard Italian swearing: *'Managia!'*

Ping! A bullet hit the bare tabletop and gouged out a splinter that flew and hit the witness in the face.

'Ouch!' she yelled, blood running down her cheek.

The suspect was now crouched low, firing randomly into the restaurant. Everyone, including Parsons and Taylor, had rushed to the kitchen or hidden behind pillars.

'I've got to get out of here,' gasped the witness. Then she did something either utterly brave or foolhardy – she stood up and launched herself at the suspect's legs in an impressive rugby tackle.

As she fell, the suspect released one more shot, which caught me in the arm.

The witness was still straddling the other woman, holding one arm up her back in a half-nelson, while the suspect wriggled and shrieked beneath her.

Parsons re-emerged from the kitchen. 'I'll arrest her, shall I, Sarge?' he asked.

'What do you think, Parsons?' I spat, nursing my arm, which hurt like hell.

Parsons strode over and, moving the witness aside, hand-cuffed the suspect and read her rights like an American TV cop, getting spat in the face for his trouble.

The witness whirled towards me, furious.

'You said...' she paused to breathe. 'You promised I'd be safe.'

She lifted her arm, swung it round and walloped me full in the face.

And that is how I got the black eye.

Fade.

A forty year old man with a Welsh accent

Wenglish

by

David Stroud

Setting

A London pub.

Man of 40, Welsh accent.

A Welsh souvenir oven glove (or similar).

Performance time:

15 minutes

Lights up. Rhodri stands facing a microphone.

Don't know why I'm here, really. I only called in for a pint last week and this whatsitsname – Open Mic – was on. With local poets and storytellers and things. They're quite good, aren't they...? I mean, if you've got nothing else to do.

They must have heard my accent. Asked me to come back to talk about the English and Welsh language, the relationship between them and...Said there'd be a couple of pints in it for me. So...here I am.

Pause.

Any Welsh people here?...Well, now might be a good time for you to go to the loo or something. Before you gets really embarrassed.

Pause.

I came up to live in London when I was in my twenties. Funny how we say 'up to London' because when you look at the map we should say across to London, *yntê*?

Anyway, what I'm going to talk to you about tonight is Wenglish. Yeah, I think that's the best way to do it. You see, I was brought up in *Cwm Tawe* – the Swansea Valley – speaking Wenglish, although it wasn't called that at the time. Of course, it was only after I came up to London that I realised that a lot of the words I used were not English, as I'd thought, but Welsh.

Take the word *crachach*, for instance, which means aristocrat or snob. Or *maldod*, which means to spoil or pamper. Or *hwyl*, meaning joy or enthusiasm. Together with my strong accent, I was asked more than once, 'Oi, mate, can ya speak English?'

I'd say things like, '*Maldod* that *crachach* wants and there's no *hwyl* in him for nothing.' To me that was perfect English. Translated into proper English that would be, 'He's an apathetic, attention-seeking snob.'

13

Pause.

For us Welsh, the word 'now' can mean now or in the future. In the valleys, there is no contradiction in saying, 'I'll do it now in a minute', or even, 'I'll do it now next week'. Well, you can imagine the confusion that caused when I came up to London.

Another word we use differently is 'after', which to us means later. Like, 'I'll see you after.' English people used to ask me, 'After what?' In the valleys we never say 'later'. Unless we want to sound like a *crachach*.

Pause.

In Wales, would you believe, the sitting-room is called the kitchen. So what do you call the kitchen? I hear you cry out. No, Clever Dick, we don't call it the sitting-room. We call it the scullery. On winter evenings we used to sit around the coal fire in the kitchen playing, 'I spies with my little eyes.'

Pause.

Now, in Wenglish many words are formed by just adding an o to the English verb. So to shop becomes *shopo*, to laugh becomes *laffo*, to smell becomes *stinco*, to be spotlessly clean becomes *spoto*...Yeah, that's it, you've got the idea. You'll all be talking like this after, I knows you will.

Pause.

One of my father's favourite words was *jib*. According to the Wenglish lexicon, *jib* can mean a) to quit, as in, 'It got difficult, so I *jibbed* it' or b) facial expression, as in, 'She's got a heck of a *jib* on her today.'

Pause.

Never thought I'd have a problem fitting in when I came up to London, though. I mean, I used to say *hylô* (that's Welsh for hello) to people when I got on the tube, and *hwyl* when I got off. But they just used to look at me as if I was something the cat had dragged in.

Pause.

My old school buttie Meno was already living in London. Said I could stay in his flat when I arrived. But when I came out of Paddington Station, no one seemed to know where 39B Mayflower Gardens was. That's Meno for you, I thought: gave me a false address he did. Lugged my suitcase around the streets for ages, looking for his place. In the end I got one of those big, black taxis to take me there. I just had no idea of how enormous London was. And the amount of people! Busier than Swansea on a Saturday night, it was.

Pause.

You're probably wondering if Meno is really a Welsh name. Well no, it's not. It's a nick-name. His real name is Dennis. You see, nick-names in Wales aren't as simple as in England where William becomes Bill, James becomes Jim, and so on. No, in Wales the nick-name is usually arrived at through several stages. Dennis. Dennis the Menace. Menace. Meno. You see? Take me, for instance – they call me Blodwyn...but I haven't quite worked that one out yet.

Pause.

I'll never forget that summer me and Meno went down to Port Eynon. Drinking all day in the Ship Inn we were. After closing time, Meno had this bright idea of skinny dipping. Lovely and warm the sea was. But when we came out...yes, you've guessed it. We couldn't find our clothes.

'I'm sure they were by here,' Meno kept saying. After running about starkers for ages, we finally gave up hope of ever finding them.

'We'll have to go to one of the chalets for help,' said Meno.

'What,' I said, 'like this?'

He beat me to the white sheet that was hanging from the clothes line, leaving me try to cover myself with... this. (*Rhodri covers his genital area with an oven glove.*)

With the sheet wrapped around him, Meno looked like the Arch Druid. The woman who opened the door of the chalet took one look at him, screamed and ran back into the bedroom. Meno stepped inside, trying to explain what had happened. Then this bloke came out of the bedroom in pyjamas.

'I've called the police,' he shouted.

'Oh, there was no need for that, *myn*,' said Meno. 'A mini cab would've been all right.'

Anyway, it worked out okay in the end. They put us up for the night. (*Pause.*) The police, I mean.

In the morning they gave us black coffee. Meno spat it out: '*Achaf fi*! Tastes like *pisio cath*!' They ignored his reference to cat's urine, but they were not amused when he asked if he could have a cappuccino instead.

'Don't use language like that with me, *boyo*,' said this copper, 'or I'll sort you out here and now.'

Pause.

You know what, I went back to visit my sister and brother-in-law last weekend. First time in years, it was. Rushed into the house to go to the *ty bach* – I mean, the toilet. Well, you know, three and a half hours on the motorway. Annwyn said, 'You'll have to go after. Geriant's in the bath.' Couldn't wait, so I dashed out the back. When I came back into the house, Geriant was shouting down the stairs, 'Annwyn, Dai next door just texted me. There's a bloke peeing on our shed!'

When I settled down with a cup of tea and a Welsh cake, Annwyn said, 'What's it like to come back after so many years, then?'

'Well,' I said, 'Penllergaer has certainly changed.'

'We don't call it that anymore,' said Geriant.

'No?'

'No. We call it The Gaer now.'

The Gaer! Can you imagine? The Gaer. Bloody *crachach*.

Pause.

16

Anyway, he said I'd come at just the right time because it was Grab a Granny Night at the British Legion Club. Now, apparently they have to double the number of bouncers every Grab a Granny Night. And put extra lighting in the bushes and trees outside to stop the pensioners' hanky panky. The chairman of the club told me, 'Worse than the bloody kids they are, *myn*!'

I saw this woman there who reminded me of a girl I knew in school, who was a couple of years older than me. Had a bit of a crush on her, I did. I used to call her *Meg Fawr*, Big Meg. One day she got stroppy and said, 'I'm not big!' and I said, 'Well, that's not what I've heard, Meg.'

Mind you, I think I must have modified my way of talking since I've been living in London, because my little Welsh goddaughter said to me, 'Can't you talk tidy like us, Fairy Godfather?'

Pause.

Hey, I can't finish without mentioning the Welshmen who like their lovers to have woolly jumpers...that don't come off. You've heard of that village in Spain, where men run for their lives in front of bulls? Have you? What's it called again?...Pamplona! That's the boy. Well, in the valleys there's one where the sheep run for their lives in front of men. Terrified, they are.

Don't want you to think I'm knocking the practice, though. After all, it's only natural, *yntê*? And it does have certain advantages. For instance, you don't have to talk afterwards. And they don't get upset if you forget their birthday. Mind you, I'm not talking from personal experience here. I've never done anything like that – could never catch one.

Waves, moving away.

– *Hwyl fawr!*

Fade.

One day ... I'll be rich

The Waiting Man

by

Stephen Baker

Setting

Derek, 55 year old man,
with slight learning difficulties.

Scene 1

A sparsely decorated bedroom.

A book shelf is the only fitting on bare walls. It is full of books from the same author, with audio tapes and DVDs neatly stacked on top of the books.

A chair is adjacent to the single bed.

Scene 2

A room in the Guildhall set up for a meeting.

Scene 3

Porter's lobby

A calendar on the wall indicates it's Monday and a clock, it's morning.

Performance time:

15 minutes

Scene One

Lights up.

Derek sits alone in his bedroom; he sits on the chair adjacent to his single bed.

I am so excited. I am waiting for the postman to bring my special parcel. I am an avid reader of books about making money and from one particular author: Theodore Wilderspin. He's a billionaire you know.

I discovered his books and audio tapes in my younger days when I was looking for direction in my life. He has brought out a new book and has personally written to me offering me the chance to purchase his new book at a special discount. Of course, I have jumped at the chance.

Points to the shelf on the wall.

I call this shelf my shelf of success. (*He gives off a wry smile.*) I have had it since childhood, it used to be filled with children's fantasy books but not anymore!

I have all of Mr Wilderspin's books and tapes, I've bought them over many years. It all started back in 1985 when I was disillusioned in my life – particularly at work.

I saw an advertisement in a newspaper at the library asking the question: Do you want to be rich beyond your wildest dreams? I thought, of course I do!

If you answered yes, the advertisement said, then you need to purchase my books and audio tapes. I purchased straight away. It cost me £25. It was the best £25 I ever spent. I got his book and cassette tapes on how to make money.

Removes a letter from his bedside table drawer and holds it up like a trophy.

Mr Wilderspin sent me this letter dated 25 April 1986, personally addressed, and he informed me that he was going to personally guide me through his 'Programme on Wealth Creation'.

He states that making money is really like baking a cake, 'you have to have all of the ingredients, to make it a success.' He explains that he will write to me periodically offering further readings and tapes all offering the missing ingredients needed to complete the Wealth Programme. I look on it a bit like doing a jigsaw puzzle. I'm like a child again waiting for my next book giving me further tips. I can't wait for the money to come rolling in.

Points once again to his shelf of success.

What I like about Mr Wilderspin is that he moves with the times. When he first started up he offered cassettes, then video tapes and now he has moved onto DVDs.

I panicked the other day when my cassette player stopped working. I took it to the shop on the High Street for repair. The young whippersnapper in there looked at it and said he was not sure if they could repair it as they may not be able to get the parts.

Bloody cheek. I soon put him in his place. That was state of the art when I bought it. It took a while, but I finally got it back working. I must purchase a DVD player, I did not want to miss the opportunity of purchasing the DVDs that Mr Wilderspin was offering so I have bought them. I think Argos are selling DVD players for £19.99, I must investigate. Don't want to miss out on the new tips he is revealing.

Can't wait for the money to come rolling in.

Father spoke to me the other day wanting me to increase my board. Something about the cost of living. I had to agree in the end. Just wait until the money starts rolling in. I may have to live here for a while until I can buy my own place.

Points to the corner of the room.

I'll start with a smart TV over there, maybe 42 inch.

Holds up an advertisement from a newspaper and points to a new TV.

That's the one for me, wall to wall sound.

Holds up the local property guide.

I've seen the house I want to buy when the money comes rolling in. It's £250,000 set in its own grounds. Won't have to worry about noisy neighbours.

Maybe it will come tomorrow. Mr Wilderspin might even be away on holiday. Maybe on his yacht, or maybe he's in the South of France. Too busy spending his money no doubt!

Laughs out loud.

Can't wait until the money starts rolling in.

Fade.

Scene Two

Lights up.

Derek sits in a room in the Guildhall. He has just been informed that his application for a swimming pool in the back garden has been rejected by the committee.

What a complete farce that was. The problem with this city is it's run by people with no ambition. I blame the socialists. They never want people to succeed. I put my application in like everyone else and expected to have a fair hearing and what happened in there was a joke!

Points to a committee room further down the hall.

My application was the first to be heard after the lunch break. I've no doubt that some of the members took the opportunity to visit the local public houses and pour alcohol down their throats like there's no tomorrow. One was so drunk that he fell off his chair when the planning officer described my application.

What is the world coming to when elected members get tanked up whilst attending a public meeting? I ask myself.

Beams a smile right across his face.

Mr Wilderspin has always said: 'Think Big' and that's what I do.
Think Big!

I used to love those trips to the seaside with mother and father. Mother used to be in her deck-chair on the beach and father and I would be jumping into the sea. So what better, than to have a swimming pool in the back garden? Now that mother and father are advancing in age it's ideal.

I see it as a dual use, mother and father could use it during the day and I could use it on an evening. Of course, I wouldn't want my parents using it when I've got my girlfriends and other executives there. Can't have my mother sat in her deck chair drinking her cocktails with a cherry on the stick when I've got people there with important matters to discuss.

I see my use of the pool as relaxation and business, which is just what Mr Wilderspin will use his for. Of course, when I buy my luxury house I'll build another swimming pool in the back garden of my new home and leave this one for my parents to use 24 hours a day.

But because of the Socialists, Liberals and the one Tory on the planning committee I am seriously delayed in my plans, I will have to submit an appeal to a planning inspector in Bristol! Could take months before this decision is overturned.

The Tories in this city have never accepted me as a member of the constituency. The first time I turned up for a meeting they didn't even have a cycle rack near the constituency office. I had to leave my bicycle in a pub car park half a mile away. What sort of carry on is that?

I want to be a candidate in the local elections. I'll send you an application pack in the post, said the chair of the constituency. Never received a thing. Total incompetence!

Why would I want to bother myself with people who can't get their act together? They'll never take over the running of the Council with that sort of performance.

Idiots!

When I finally do receive my application pack I'll be on my way onto the Council. They won't know what's hit them. I'll show the idiots how to debate. These idiots I currently work with are no match for me, so how are the Socialists and the wet Liberals going to fare?

I read the quality papers, not the Red Tops like my illustrious colleagues. When I won the argument with one of my colleagues, he threatened to take me outside and quote: punch my lights out, unquote. Typical language and actions of a blue collar worker.

Moron!

When I finally get my application form and get elected I'll take local politics by storm. I've even chosen the pin stripe suit that I'll be wearing for the council meetings and when the Lord Mayor calls out 'Councillor Williams to speak,' up I'll get and show them all what they've been missing. The Constituency Chair will be in the public gallery and she will be amazed at my knowledge and debating skills. When you read the broadsheets and law books, as I do, you can't help but broaden your knowledge.

Puts his hand to the side of his mouth. Whispers.

I bought a fascinating law book the other Sunday from a car boot sale, have read it from cover to cover. *British Law in 1972 New Legislation* it's called. Never mind this modern rubbish. This is the real McCoy.

Modern lawyers just don't know what they are talking about. You wait until I get on the Council and the Planning Committee. They'll all be staggered at my grasp of legislation and never mind that nonsense 'The Local Plan' which all the councillors on the Planning Committee seem to think they have to refer to – as they did with my application, I'll vote in favour of any application if the applicant has ambition.

Thinking Big, as Mr Wilderspin says, has its own rewards.

Fade.

Scene Three

Lights up.

Derek sits alone in the Porter's lobby. He clutches a white A4 envelope and holds it aloft.

Inside this envelope lies my future. I saw the advertisement for Head of Geography Department. I hurried along to the Human Resource office on Friday and made sure I got me application given to me so I could spend the weekend completing it. I'm on first name terms with the young girl in there. 'Hello Derek,' she said when I appeared. 'Hello Jayne,' I said.

Laughs as he describes the encounter.

'Which job are you interested in this time,' she said. 'Reference 2380,' I said. Knowing the reference number always impresses you know. I filled it in over the weekend and am handing it in today.

I tried to have an informal chat with the named contact on the application form, but when I went to her office she looked up at me and informed me that she was rather on the busy side and advised that I should just submit my application. So I have.

References are always a bit tricky. I use my tutor at my night class and my line manager. At least they understand that some people don't want to stay put in their lives. When I saw my line manager about giving me a reference she said: 'I won't stand in your way Derek,' as she was rushing to yet another meeting. Always busy these sorts of people.

I would have gone for her job when it was advertised and no doubt I would have got it, but I did not fancy overseeing the morons who would be my subordinates. It's bad enough working alongside them never mind overseeing them! I always get my line managers to give me a reference. They know someone who's going places and who isn't. Five managers there's been in this department, and all have been impressed with me to give a reference, no quibble. Eventually this will pay off.

If at first you don't succeed try, try again. As my mother used to say.

The other guys I work with just don't understand that people like me need to get on. They have sent me to Coventry because they feel I have, as one guy told me, 'Delusions of grandeur' which is just not true.

Sure I don't eat in the staff canteen but why should I? I eat in Staff House with all the senior officers. I'm not bringing a packed lunch like the other porters. They sit there in the canteen eating their packed lunch and reading the only newspapers available in there – the Red Tops.

Not for me.

I read the broadsheets and Mr Wilderspin said in one of his books that if you want success then you should only mix with successful people. Which is why I eat my lunch in Staff House and why I always sit at the table usually occupied by the senior officers.

I think they are really impressed as to how I converse with them. I always inform them all of the latest book that I am reading from my night class. The lecturers particularly seem impressed with my reading matter.

I always try to make everyone aware as to how well read I am. One of my tasks is to take books to the relevant department. I always read a section or two from one of the books before I set off. Then when I reach the department and see one of the academics I am able to converse with them on the subject matter. I can tell they are really impressed with my knowledge.

I have just written the first draft of my first book and have taken the liberty of dropping off a copy with a lecturer in the Literature Department. Not sure when she will get back to me with comments. They are very busy people these academics, like Mr Wilderspin, always doing something or other.

I have spoken to the secretary of the department and she always says that she is a very busy person and will get back to me when she can.

Hope it's soon.

But, last week as I was eating my lunch there was a bit of an issue. A new person started in a post that I applied for.

Okay, I did not get an interview, she obviously did, and was able to impress on the panel as to how good she was. I did not get this opportunity. But I am not bitter.

Good luck to her.

But, last week I sat at the table, as I generally do, and she sat opposite me. Spent most of the time staring at me. Whether she knew that I had applied for the same post as her I don't know, but it was a bit uncomfortable to say the least.

I was engaging with an officer as to the role of the porter, as he had asked me what I did on campus. When out of the blue she said that she'd heard that a new porter had started work called Walter Mitty and she asked if I knew of this chap.

This seemed to amuse everyone on the table. I quietly replied that I did not and that maybe he was one of the new starters in another department.

I ask myself...Am I expected to know everyone who works on campus?

Fade.

Just kept it inside

A True Gentleman

by

John Samson

Winner, Harrow Writers' Circle Monologue Competition
2017

Setting

Mary, a woman in her late seventies suffering from early signs of dementia

Mary stands at the top of a staircase holding the railings. She stares down to the bottom of the stairs, a concerned look on her face.

Performance time:

10 minutes

Lights up.

Is he all right?

It's that large Jamaican nurse down there. I like her. She is kind, always smiling and laughing. Rita. That's her name. Rita. 'Like Bob Marley's wife,' she tells everyone. I don't know who Bob Marley is and Rita laughs when I say that she must introduce me to Mr Marley one day.

Changes to a bad Jamaican accent.

'Oh Mr Marley he be long gone now. Long gone.' Rita says. I love the way she speaks, 'he be long gone'. She says that when people die, 'Mr Patterson he be gone now.' Sometimes, like when Daphne Silverstone went, she says that the person 'pass'.

'Mrs Daphne, she pass last night all peaceful like in her sleep,' Rita told us the next day.

She cares though does our Rita. She really cares. You can see it when she tells you that another one has died. There is sadness in her eyes when someone pass. Most of the other staff don't seem to care much. I remember when...

Pauses to think, then becomes frustrated as she can't recall.

They say I've got dementia, that's why I can't remember everything. Early stage dementia, they say. Sometimes I hear them talking quietly, they think that because my mind is going that I am also deaf, but I hear them.

'Didn't recognise her granddaughter today.' I don't know if they are talking about me. I'm not the only one here with it. Henry across the way (*She indicates with a nod of her head.*) he's much further along than me. Lies in bed all day he does, staring at the ceiling. No wonder he can't remember his granddaughter, the ceilings in here can do that to a person, they are horrible, they do something to your mind. It must have been Henry they were talking about when they said, 'Didn't even recognise his granddaughter today...her granddaughter.'

She stares blankly for a second, frustration increasing, then snaps out of it and peers down the stairs.

Is he okay? She is looking for a pulse, is Rita. She is a nurse after all.

That's Ron Baldwin down there at the bottom of the stairs. He's not moving, lying at a strange angle. He can't be comfortable lying like that.

Ron is a true gentleman. Moved in here in the Autumn. Sprightly. A widower. And handsome. (*She gives a knowing smile.*) He was hot property. A true gentleman, all the women loved him. Even charmed the nurses with his Eton accent and cravats and handkerchief peaking out the top of his jacket pocket. Always well dressed. Looks quite dashing in his blue sports coat, quite dashing. Reminded me of...

She puzzles for a moment.

I was married once. But he died, my husband. Two months after he retired. Just fell down dead and left me. We had plans for our retirement. We were going to travel. Spain, The Algarve. Maybe even America. New York. The Statue of Liberty. Central Park. Grand Central Station. But he went and died on me. Heart attack they told me. You should have seen his face when his heart attacked him. He had this look as if to say, 'This should not be happening to me. Not yet.' Surprised both of us if the truth be told. Worked really hard so I didn't see much of him, but I still missed him when he was gone...miss him. He was a comfort to have around. He sorted out paying all the bills and all those sorts of things. I never even knew how to use one of those automatic cash machine thingies. He looked after me like that. You'd think I would remember his name...

It's in here somewhere (*Points to her head.*)...I just can't access it. They say I've got dementia. Early stages. But it still frustrates me some days. I could ask Rita what my husband's name was, but she is busy with Mr Baldwin.

Is he okay?

She gets no reply but still stares down the stairs for a good while, concentrating. Then suddenly she smiles.

Jeremy! I told you it was in there. (*Taps the side of her head.*) I'm not totally gone just yet. Jeremy.

She processes a few memories that make her smile, then becomes frustrated as her memory fails.

Darn it. They're in there, the memories. I know they are there but it's like British Rail. There are delays, the wrong kind of leaves on the tracks. (*She smiles.*) The wrong kind of memories on the track.

She looks away from the audience, ashamed of the memories.

Jeremy. He was good to me. Gentle. Kind.

I never thought that I would get married. Not after...well, you now...not after what happened. But then I met Jeremy. We were close at first, like any married couple. Close at first, then you slowly drift apart without even knowing you are doing so. There was never any animosity or disagreement or anything like that, we just got used to each other being there but we were living our own lives. I was always grateful to him.

She looks away, embarrassed by a memory, then looks down the stairs as if to change the subject.

It doesn't look good for Mr Baldwin, Rita's called for help, that can't be good. He was a true gentleman, Mr Baldwin. I must confess that I took quite a fancy to him. And I think that he liked me too. I think that there was a bond there. We would have tea together in the morning. They don't know how to make it properly in this place, too weak. But beggars can't be choosers.

Mr Baldwin, Ron, he never complained, but you could see it in his face when he drank his tea. Like he was drinking cod liver oil. Never said anything, though. And the biscuits this morning were stale. The weather was nice, the biscuits not. We were sitting in the common room and the sun was shining. Warm enough that he took off that smart sports jacket that he always wore. I didn't expect him to be wearing a short sleeved shirt, I had always pictured him as a long sleeve man. I didn't expect...

She looks at the audience, wondering if she can trust them with her story.

I never reported it. Never told anyone at the time. Not my mum, not my best friend, Alison. Definitely not my dad. Not even Jeremy when we got married. I could never tell him. Just kept it inside. But you do don't you. You clean yourself up and get on with your life. Try to box up that memory and hide it away in your mind. But where was the dementia when you really needed it. I tried to forget what happened. But these things stay with you. They never go away, even the dementia is not helping. I will remember those hands tearing at my blouse, pushing up my skirt, knees forcing my legs apart, hot breath on my neck and hands pulling, pushing, pinching, demanding. Hands. Hands. Hands. There were others. I remember hearing laughter, rough voices. 'Give it to her! Let her have it!'

What have I done? Why are they doing this to me. I tried to scream, it's hard to scream when there's a knife at your throat. 'Stop struggling or you'll get hurt.' I couldn't see faces, just hands and the knife...and an arm. An arm with a tattoo. A tattoo of a cartoon dog with 'Binky' written underneath. It's funny how a detail like that stayed while other memories left.

She stops and smoothes her skirt down as if getting up from the ordeal again.

I went to the Police Station, but lost my nerve. How could I tell them what had happened? How could I tell anyone? I just went home and cleaned myself up. Tried to pack those memories away.

She stares down the stairs again.

It was warm in the common room this morning and he took his sports coat off did our Mr Baldwin.

Pause.

He's gone now. Rita has pulled the blanket over his face. It's sad. The stairs in the place are a hazard. They need to do something about them. Better railings perhaps? Mr Baldwin be gone now, Rita. Oh yes, Rita, he and his tattoo of 'Binky', he certainly be gone now.

Pause.

It's funny. Life that is. One moment you're talking to someone at the top of the stairs, the next moment they're tumbling down. Lost his footing. I heard his neck crack. He be gone now, ow Mr Baldwin. He be gone.

She looks up and a knowing smile spreads across her face.

Fade.

He was kind man

'Kenneth'

by

Barbara Towell

Character

Carla, middle aged woman, works as an accountant for Ferguson International.

Setting

A modern day Accounts office in a large company, Ferguson International.
There are two desks and chairs in the office opposite one another.

Properties:
laptop
office phone
cup of coffee
handbag with mobile phone
small photograph
pocket diary
umbrella

Performance time:

approximately 20 minutes

Lights up.

Carla sits at desk working on laptop in an office. Her eyes are on the monitor screen. Opposite is an unoccupied chair and desk.

Kenneth, do you have...Oh my God! Of course not. (*Pause.*) It's hard to believe Kenneth isn't here anymore. So strange seeing his desk empty.

Sighs. Gets up. Walks to centre stage. Faces audience.

The thing is, (*Points to desk opposite.*) Kenneth was always there – ever since I started in Accounts – part of the furniture so to speak – at that desk by the window – beavering away – every morning – even before I'd got my toe through the door.

Walks to her desk. Sits down. Faces audience.

Pause.

God! We must've shared this office for around fifteen years. I can picture him, sitting over there, every lunch time saying the very same thing: 'I wonder what Samantha has put in my sandwiches today?' And you know what? Some days when I looked at those neat little triangular sandwiches and the slice of home-made cake, I felt...almost guilty, thinking about the cheesy door-steps I'd stuck into Terry's hand at 7 a.m.

Pause.

Kenneth was what you'd call a 'nice' man. I mean, he'd insist in giving me one of his sandwiches when I forgot my lunch. Yes, he was – a really nice man.

Pause.

And well turned out too. Shirts, always perfectly ironed – by Samantha no doubt. Made me think of the creases I always ignore when I iron Terry's shirts. And sometimes, just some-times, I felt like killing Samantha – Samantha the Stepford wife – for letting the side down. Note I said, 'Almost felt guilty.' Be-cause I reminded myself, that she was, after all, a full-time housewife with only Kenneth and their son Peter to look after.

Pause.

They were happy – Kenneth and Samantha. And it is reassuring to know there are some couples who are genuinely happy – and not just ones on the telly. Mind you, in soaps these days they're barely married before divorce is on the cards. Well, not Kenneth and Samantha.

Pause.

On the other hand, you never quite know who's happy and who's not. No one really knows the truth – what goes on behind closed doors. How often do you read about a man – or some-times a woman – disappearing, disappearing without trace? No warning – none at all. The partner comes home one day and poof they've gone. Bags packed – no note, nothing. Shocked, the partner tells everyone they haven't a clue why – thought everything was hunkydory. Amazing! (*Pause.*) I wonder how Terry would feel if I took off one day without a word?

Pause.

You never actually think you're going to miss people until they're gone, do you? Time marches on and we take them for granted. It was like that with good old Kenneth. Actually he wasn't *old* Kenneth. Probably only in his late forties, or early fifties. Anyway, one minute I'm saying to him, 'Have a nice weekend.' And the next he's dropped down dead! Yes, dropped down dead, (*Points to the window.*) right out there in the car park, three days ago.

Pause.

Who would have thought I'd miss him? Now don't misunderstand me. I wasn't harbouring some secret passion for him. No. I just liked working with him. You get used to people, don't you? Then there was his family. Hearing what they'd got up to. I liked that. The little everyday things – how him and Samantha got on at the pub quiz; and Peter helping with decorating the outside of the house and dropping half the paint from the top of the ladder. And of course those fantastic holidays to Italy. It felt as if I knew them in an odd sort of way. (*Looks at watch.*) Oh my God! Look at the time. Better not sit here doing nothing; so much work to do – double the accounts! Yes, I do miss you Kenneth.

Lights fade down.

Fade up.

Carla picks up cup of coffee from her desk, is about to drink when her mobile phone 'pings'. She puts down cup, takes out mobile phone from her bag and reads the text message. She frowns, sighs and then turns phone off. Turns and speaks to audience.

A text from Terry. Do I mind if he goes to an away match this weekend? Well, actually I do. I mind very much. I'd been hoping, since Sally will be home from uni this weekend that the three of us would go for a Chinese meal Saturday – after all it is her birthday.

Sighs. Looks down and is about to start work on laptop when she looks up and turns to audience.

Hey! I guess I shouldn't really complain. All in all, guess Terry's not a bad husband – I suppose you'd say we are much like most couples, chug along okay – most of the time.

Pause.

Bet Samantha and Kenneth didn't just chug along.

Pause.

I wonder if she called him Ken. Ken, in those moments...You know what I mean. (*Chuckles.*)

Pause.

I wasn't going to say anything, but I will. Terry and I had this massive row last night – so I'm sure you'll understand, what with that and Kenneth dying, I'm a bit out of sorts today. I'm sure you get it. (*Pause.*) Well, to be frank, that's what the row was about...him...him not getting it – getting it enough that is. Anyway...bet Samantha and Kenneth didn't row about that. Mind you, (*Chuckles to herself.*) it's hard to imagine Kenneth...let's not go down that route... (*Phone on desk rings.*) Certainly Mr Bradshaw. Yes, yes, they'll be ready by three thirty. I will bring them to you myself, no problem. (*Puts down phone.*)

Now that I'm being honest, sometimes it was a bit much – got up my nose. And I asked myself, did Kenneth and Samantha *ever* exchange harsh words? Did Peter ever turn round and say: 'Fuck off!'? Well, I guess he must've sometimes. But, you know what? Kenneth would never have admitted it. (*Pause.*) Suppose, looking back, I was a bit envious. I mean you don't want to have perfection rubbed in your face, do you? Especially when the best thing you've done all weekend was to watch *Casualty* on the box. And yes, it would be lovely at the weekends to picnic by the sea or walk in Bluebell Wood. Lucky Samantha and Peter having Kenneth. Well...

Pause.

Lights dim.

Fade up.

Carla walks from her desk to the one opposite and picks up a pocket diary lying on the floor. She faces the audience.

41

HR couldn't wait to clear Kenneth's desk. I offered to do it, but Mr Bradshaw said: *(imitates Mr Bradshaw's voice.)* Oh no, Carla! You can't do it. HR has to do that – all part of Data Protection.

(Carla's own voice.) Well, anyway, it was all done in such a great hurry – everything was just thrown into a box. And guess what? She managed to drop Kenneth's diary on the floor and not even notice.

Opens diary and finds a small photo. She places diary on desk and then looks more closely at photo.

My God! It's odd finding this here. *(Addressing audience.)* You see, years ago I asked Kenneth if he could bring in some photos of the family. Said he wasn't much into taking photos, but would, once he'd bought a decent camera. I reminded him from time to time, but he didn't – not for ages. Then one Monday morning he brought a photo in. It came as a real surprise. He told me that a friend of the family had taken it that Sunday when they'd all gone for a boat trip on the Serpentine. That was the only time I got to see a photo of Peter – and here it is. *(Looks at photo.)* A really cute smile – and that wonderful thatch of blond hair. Gorgeous blue eyes. 'He'll steal the girls' hearts,' I told Kenneth. That didn't go down too well. *(Examining photo more closely.)* You can see it from the photo – intelligent as well as good looking – ended up with a million A grades. Kenneth said Peter was a chip off the old block – like his mother – bright and beautiful. A funny way to describe your wife as an old block, but that's what he said; more than once – a chip off the old block. But fair is fair, Kenneth wasn't bad looking himself – in that slightly old fashioned way – you know, like Cary Grant in those old films.

Pause.

Anyway, soon after the photo of Peter appeared, I asked, 'Why don't you bring in a photo of Samantha? Put it on your desk. You know, like Mr Bradshaw has of his wife?'

'I told you, Carla, I'm not much into photos,' he replied. 'Besides when you've got the real thing at home you don't need a photo at work reminding you of what your wife looks like.' In a way I suppose, he had a point. (*Pause.*) However, I do have an idea of what Samantha looks like. Because one day, when Mandeep from General Office was in here having lunch with me, we were chatting about some of those really ancient TV shows, and she asked me if I'd ever seen *Bewitched*. I said, I had and thought it quite dated, but amusing – what with Samantha twitching her nose to cast spells. We were laughing and saying if only we could do that, our lives would be very different. And then to our surprise Kenneth looks up from his *Guardian* and says he likes the programme too, and that Samantha the witch, looks so much like his wife.' I must confess, I'd never imagined Kenneth's wife to be a cute, sexy blonde somehow. 'She's not a witch of course,' he adds. I think he was making a joke. Mandeep and I made an effort to laugh anyway. (*Sighs.*) Oh Kenneth! Kenneth you were a nice man.

Puts photo on desk and picks up diary. Flicks through pages.

Nothing in it, except his name and address on the first page – 45, Westbury Avenue, West Ealing. Oh! And here on the back page – Samantha's birthday, June 10th – and Peter's, December 6th. Wedding Anniversary, April 20th.

Quickly flicks through pages again. Then takes photo from desk and slips it inside the diary and puts it in her pocket. Returns to desk and begins to work on laptop.

Lights dim.

Quickly fade up.

When I started here at Ferguson International, Kenneth and I barely spoke – other than about work of course. But I'm quite a chatty person, as no doubt you've noticed. So gradually after a month or two he opened up a bit.

Pause.

I still remember the day he first mentioned Peter. It was my Sally's fifth birthday and I told Kenneth I'd be having that afternoon off – you know for her party. And that's when he told me he had a son – more or less the same age as Sally. Anyway, I could sense straight away Peter was the apple of his eye. Well, I mean who wouldn't be proud if their five year old could spell words like er – hyacinth?

Pause.

'Course then some years later he won that scholarship to St. Paul's – the public school. Over the moon he was. And then there was the cricket, the lad being so good at cricket.

Pause.

Don't get me wrong, Kenneth didn't boast. The way he said it, didn't sound like boasting at all. He wasn't like that. Just told me – with a kind of a glow. And I was pleased for the lad. And for Kenneth. After all, Kenneth didn't seem to have much else in his life other than Peter – and of course Samantha. I mean most men talk about football, maybe cars, music, DIY or whatever, but not him.

Pause.

Then when Sally got into York to study History, Peter got into medical school – Addenbrooks in Cambridge. I can tell you, Kenneth was beside himself with joy...and who could blame him? He had every right to be a proud father. (*Pause.*) Poor Peter. What a shock – to hear out of the blue your dad's died of a heart attack. And what about Samantha? Oh God!

Lights dim.

Lights fade up.

Enter Carla.

No funeral. There's to be no funeral. That came as a bombshell. Kenneth, apparently, wants his body to go to medical research. In his will, Mr Bradshaw said. You see, when I handed him the diary, I asked him when the funeral was likely to take place. And then he told me. Perhaps Kenneth decided that because Peter's going into medicine. (*Carla gives cynical chuckle.*) You should have seen his face – Mr Bradshaw's face that is, as he suddenly clammed up and refused to give me any more information. Said it's against the Data Protection Act! I ask you, the guy's dead for God's sake!

Pause.

Anyway, not very comforting for Samantha, thinking about her husband being dissected, is it?

Lights dim.

Lights fade up after about 20 seconds.

Carla enters wearing a coat. Shakes wet umbrella.

What a weekend it was. And I'm not just talking about the rain. (*Phone rings. Carla answers it.*) Um, yes, Mr Bradshaw I will do my best. Haven't had a chance yet. – Yes, as soon as possible.

Puts down phone, making a grimace at it. Takes off coat and hangs it on the back of her chair. Sits and stares into audience for a second or two.

Neither am I talking about Terry actually giving up his football match in favour of taking myself and Sally out for that Chinese meal. Nevertheless, I have to say, Terry certainly has redeemed himself in my eyes. Ten out of ten. Worth rewarding, (*Winks.*) I'd say. However, that's not what I meant when I said, 'What a weekend!'

Gets up. Walks over to desk opposite. Sits on edge. Speaks to audience.

Imagine this. It's Sunday morning. Terry and I are having a lie in – cuddled up together for a change. But while I'm lying there being deafened by the squawking magpies outside, I'm not really thinking about Terry. I'm thinking about Kenneth. Well, not really Kenneth, but Samantha; and decide to write to her – you know a letter of condolence.

Pause.

So after breakfast, I get out the writing paper – sit there...and sit there...I don't know what to write. Although I feel as if I know Samantha, I don't, not at all; and knowing Kenneth, I doubt if she knew much, if anything about me. I begin to write: Dear Samantha, Please accept my condolences...No, that's so stuffy. Should I say: I was very fond of your husband? – No – she might get the wrong idea. And then I stop, think to myself, I might as well drive over to Ealing. No problem, I remember the address. It's only about half an hour away. I can speak to Samantha face to face – and, and – say whatever feels right at the time. Yes, I decide, that's best.

Pause.

Anyway, it's still raining when I arrive at Westbury Avenue. The detached houses are Victorian in style – large and generally well maintained. I'm feeling nervous as I hurry along the pavement and wonder if it wasn't a bit foolhardy coming here. Then I'm there – at number 45. I'm surprised to see the paint work is a little worse for wear, but the front garden is impressive – immaculate. I press the doorbell, now hoping no one's home. But they are. I hear footsteps – a chain being undone. The door opens and there she is...but...she is nothing like I'd expected.

There, before me is this rather hunched, old woman. I ask to speak to Samantha Lawson.

'Samantha Lawson?' she repeats in some kind of eastern European accent.

'Yes, Kenneth Lawson's wife...er widow?' She's staring at me – her face wrinkled with confusion. 'I have come to the right house? Kenneth Lawson's?'

'He live in house, yes,' she replies, 'but not this Samantha you speak of."

Pause.

Surely, they couldn't have been divorced or separated without me knowing...or could they?

I introduce myself. And the next thing I hear her say is – that the house belongs to her. And yes, Mr Lawson had lived there – but the house belongs to her – Mrs Pilenska, Mr Lawson's landlady. He was her lodger. Her lodger for twenty-four years!

'What about Samantha and Peter?' I ask.

To cut a long story short, it turns out there is no Samantha, never was. No Peter, there never was. 'So what about all those wonderful weekends away? – And his amazing holidays?' I hear myself blurt out.

'This, I know nothing,' Mrs Pilenska says. 'Mr Lawson, I tell you, was lodger. Rented two rooms upstairs at back of house. Mostly, he stay in rooms. No one comes, no woman, no boy. Sometime he go out Saturday evening, I think, maybe, to pub. Sometime he tell me, he go visit his father, somewhere I think in north. But this not so very often.

Pause.

And soon I'm apologising for troubling her and begin turning when she says: 'But before you go, I tell you this thing. Mr Lawson, he was kind man; he cut grass behind house and look after gardens. He refuse money. I do not like this, so we have

47

arrangement. He do garden, I make him sandwiches for lunches and bake him good Polish cake each week. Otherwise, we keep to ourselves.'

Gets up from chair, walks to front of centre stage. Faces audience.

I'm gobsmacked. Totally gobsmacked. No Samantha. And bloody hell, no Peter. No wonder the lad was too good to be true – because he wasn't!

Pause.

All those years, and I never suspected the truth. Don't you think it's sad – incredibly, bloody sad, that an intelligent, nice – ordinary – grown man – in this day and age – could be so lonely that he needed to invent the perfect family. It just goes to show – the masks people wear. And no one knows what's behind them.

Lights down.

The score is...

Football Results

by
Melville Lovatt

Setting

Tess, a woman in her fifties

Performance time:

8 minutes

Lights up.

Loud Match Of The Day *music blares out.*

Music fades.

Pause.

TESS sits, wearing dressing gown and stiletto shoes.
She finishes cup of coffee, addresses audience.

The so called experts say as people get older, they tend to dream more. Tend to have lots more dreams.

Well, my husband, Dennis, is dreaming more but he tends to always have the *same* dream.

Pause.

The dream only started when he retired about nine months ago. No, it's nearly a year.

Before then, he never seemed to have dreams at all.

Now it seems he's making up for lost time.

Pause.

I wouldn't mind so much if he'd just keep quiet.

If he'd just...well, keep his dream to himself.

The trouble is, *he commentates as he dreams.*

She stands.

In the dream, he's a football commentator and player.

I've heard this dream so many times now, I can almost recite it line for line. The match has nearly finished when the dream starts. Time's running out. It goes something like this:

(*Imitating DENNIS'S north country voice.*) Now it's Cantona.

Edwards. Edwards to Charlton. Through pass from Charlton finds Ryan Giggs. Giggs to Best. Best to Rooney.

ROONEY...HE'S THROUGH! ROONEY SHOOTS!

OH THE WOODWORK'S SAVED ARSENAL AGAIN!

But make no mistake, it's all Manchester United.

Arsenal are desperately trying to hold on.

Jack Kelsey has saved them time and time again.

It's amazing the score is still nil-nil.

Just three minutes left. Arsene Wenger's on his feet.

He's pointing to his watch. Badly wants this to end.

Now United are making a substitution! Whose coming on now?

It's Dennis Higginbottom! United's new signing from Skipton Town! It's his first time out but *can he make a difference?* The clock is ticking.

Only ninety seconds left. Now it's Law. Law crosses.

Kelsey punches it away. But straight to Ronaldo just outside the box. Through pass from Ronaldo.

A neat flick from Law to Cantona. Cantona back to Ronaldo.

Arsenal just can't seem to get possession at all.

Ronaldo...OH RONALDO'S GONE DOWN!

THAT LOOKED LIKE A VERY BAD TACKLE FROM GEORGE!

Ronaldo's in pain. He's writhing on the ground.

Sir Alex is incandescent with rage. IT'S A RED CARD!

YES, GEORGE IS SHOWN THE RED CARD!

CHARLIE GEORGE FOR ARSENAL HAS BEEN SENT OFF!

Ronaldo, meanwhile, seems very badly hurt.

The stretcher's coming on. No! They're waving it away!

Ronaldo's getting up. He's back on his feet!

An *amazing* recovery, one has to say. Yes.

Arsene Wenger is livid, pacing up and down, but all his protests are falling on deaf ears.

Now it's Higginbottom to take the free kick.

This *has* to be the last kick of the match. Higginbottom shoots! IT'S GONE IN OFF THE POST!

UNITED ARE PREMIERSHIP CHAMPIONS AGAIN!

HIGGINBOTTOM'S FREE KICK GAVE KELSEY NO CHANCE!

Some say he's the best free kick taker since Beckham and after this, who would doubt it? Not me. Sir Alex Ferguson's gamble's paid off. United's fans are chanting *one* name.

HIGGINBOTTOM! They're chanting. HIGG--IN--BOTTOM! HIGG--IN--BOTTOM!

(*Own voice.*) That's when he wakes up.

Pause.

Tess briefly stares ahead.

I expect this commentary's left you asking certain questions.

How could Ronaldo play in the same team as Duncan Edwards and Dennis Law? How could Arsene Wenger be managing Jack Kelsey and Charlie George playing in the same team?

Well, the answer is this is fantasy football according to Dennis Higginbottom. Right?

I just wish, sometimes, he'd have *other* fantasies.

Pause.

Is this too much to ask?

Pause.

A bit of affection? Now and again? Sex? I'd be better off as a Nun.

Shakes head, sadly.

It's beginning to look like separate bedrooms.

Ah, well...worse things happen at sea.

Pause.

Come to think of it, I *met* Dennis at sea.

He was working as a photographer on the cruise ships.

I was a singer. A singer of sorts. Nothing much.

I was just...just a chorus singer. I was part of the cruise ship's entertainment team.

Pause.

In those days, Dennis was really quite dashing.

He looked...yes, he *did* look quite distinguished, then.

He used to have such a lovely head of hair...

Now he's left without a strand. As bald as a coot.

What I've never understood is for years we've been told bald men are supposed to be sexier. Right?

They're supposed to have more...what's the word? *Testosterone.*

If you ask me, this is just a big myth. A big myth put around by bald headed men to make us think they're God's gift. Right?

I wouldn't mind betting it's the other way around.

It's the guys who still have their hair who...

Yes, well, as I was saying, that's where I met Dennis.

He came to take a photo of the entertainment team.

In those days he was considered quite a catch.

There were quite a few girls who wouldn't have said no...

But that was *then.* That's all in the past.

I've got to deal with Dennis as he is *now.*

His main interest in bed is football. Right?

(*Decidedly.*) So this calls for a *different* approach...

She blows whistle. Holds up a red card.

Quick Fade.

Lights up.

(*Despondent.*) Well, my new Man U shirt, matching suspenders, stockings and bra didn't set the bed alight.

A peck on the cheek, then he just fell asleep!

Still, before he fell asleep, I *did* get a quick cuddle.

I haven't been getting any cuddles at all.

I suppose that's a step in the right direction?

Pause.

What do you think?

Pause.

I suppose you're thinking this is just...pathetic.

If he no longer finds me attractive...well...there's *still* plenty other fish in the sea...

Why don't I just leave? Go find someone else?

(*Despondent.*) That's easier said than done.

Pause.

Besides, I suppose I still love the sod.

God knows why. I'm sure *I* don't. I just know I *do.*

But I don't...don't want to carry on like *this.*

Tonight we'll have a talk. A *serious* talk.

(*Decidedly.*) If we can't sort this out, I'll call it a day.

If we can't sort this out, I'll leave him.

Quick fade.

Lights up.

Well, you could have knocked me down with a feather!

I swear I will never understand men.

'It's not that I didn't find you sexy', he said.

Your Man U gear really *did* turn me on, but it's just...well, it's just...I just *can't* do it.

I can't bring myself to screw my own team'!

Quick Fade.

Lights up.

Tess stands, opening her gown to reveal Arsenal shirt with white knickers and suspenders.

This new Arsenal gear feels pretty good.

The knickers are a little bit skimpy, but still...
For tonight's match Man United have made a team change.
Higginbottom's on from the start...

She winks, briefly smiles.

Loud Match Of The Day *music.*

Blackout.